James Cotter Morison

Irish Grievances

Shortly Stated

James Cotter Morison

Irish Grievances
Shortly Stated

ISBN/EAN: 9783744717335

Printed in Europe, USA, Canada, Australia, Japan

Cover: Foto ©ninafisch / pixelio.de

More available books at **www.hansebooks.com**

IRISH GRIEVANCES

SHORTLY STATED.

BY

JAMES COTTER MORISON, M.A. Oxon.

"If I were an Irishman I would be a rebel."—*Reported words of*
SIR JOHN MOORE.

"When popular discontents have been very prevalent, it may well
be affirmed and supported that there has been generally something
found amiss in the constitution or in the conduct of the Government.
The people have no interest in disorder. When they do wrong, it is
their error, not their crime. But with the governing part of the State
it is far otherwise : they certainly may act ill by design as well as by
mistake." BURKE's *Thoughts on the Cause of the Present Discontents.*

London :

LONGMANS, GREEN, READER, & DYER.

1868.

LONDON:
R. CLAY, SON, AND TAYLOR, PRINTERS
BREAD STREET HILL.

TO THE READER.

THE writer of the following pages feels that he cannot allow the ridicule which frequently attaches to a palinode to deter him from remarking that the sentiments here expressed are in many respects opposed to the tenor of an article he wrote in the January number of the *Fortnightly Review*. That article was the too hasty expression of a set of opinions that sprang, in great measure, from national prejudice, from an inadequate knowledge —which he may perhaps also qualify as national— of the actual grievances of Ireland, and from insufficient meditation on their causes past and present. A visit to Ireland, extending over several weeks, and devoted to the exclusive study of Ireland and her history, has wrought in the writer's mind a grave change of convictions. He

B

deems it at least fairly presumable, that opinions which are the result of conscientious and painstaking inquiry are more likely to be correct than those which he formerly held (and which he observes many of his countrymen still hold) with little inquiry or none. This perhaps reasonable presumption has induced him to write the following pamphlet and submit it to the candour of the public.

IRISH GRIEVANCES

SHORTLY STATED.

THE dangerous but still the only working phase
which our policy now ever assumes with regard to
questions of first-rate importance, "that something
must be done," appears to have been reached in
reference to Ireland. Most slowly, most reluct-
antly, English public opinion has been brought to
perceive that Ireland is far from being that prospe-
rous improving country which it was so agree-
able to think her. An heroic resistance was made
before the pleasing hallucination was allowed to
vanish. Even yet it has not vanished universally.
With many persons, even yet, an object of paramount necessity is "not to attach too much importance to Fenianism and Irish disaffection," and it is
suggested, by a process of reasoning not very clear,

B 2

that not facts but their recognition is likely to prove dangerous to the State. However, this language is now acknowledged to be held in obedience to the primary duty of not alarming the public mind—a heinous offence, apparently, when committed. Short of doing anything so wicked as alarming the public mind, most speakers and writers now admit that the state of matters in Ireland is very grave indeed. It is no longer asserted, as it lately was—with amazing vehemence if the fact were so—that "Fenianism has nothing in it." But, on the contrary, it is confessed that a more subtle, insidious, and far-reaching danger has seldom threatened the country. Public opinion, although of course not alarmed, is thoroughly excited. Mysterious and wearisome as Irish questions have long been voted to be, it is felt that they must resolutely be faced once more. An Irish session has begun in the House of Commons, and the habitual apathy of Englishmen to Ireland and her affairs is replaced by emotions of a very different character.

For indeed it has come to this: that we, the great exemplars and almost the inventors of civil and religious liberty, as we flattered ourselves, are reduced to holding an integral portion of our empire in subjection to our authority solely by means of

military force. We, who have preached constitutional government to every creature in season and
out of season, are forced to deprive six millions of
our fellow-citizens of its privileges and safeguards.
There are, doubtless, many among us who regard
Irish disaffection simply as an intolerable and
never-ending nuisance : but there are many likewise
—and their number, it may be hoped, is growing—
who regard it also as an intolerable disgrace. The
question which many Englishmen now ask themselves is not only, Are we able, but, Ought we to
be willing to hold Ireland solely by means of our
superior strength ? For, in spite of sneers to the
contrary, England has a conscience whose dictates
she will obey if you can only touch it : a slow process, no doubt, but one which has been successfully
achieved more than once. Did we not go without
sugar to our tea, rather than encourage slavery after
we had become convinced of its wickedness ; and
did we not commercially ruin our West Indian
possessions, besides keeping up a chronic risk of war
with Spain and America, for the same object ? The
English conscience, with reference to Ireland, is
dull because it is unenlightened ; Irish grievances
are not redressed, because they are not realized or
even believed in. Differences of race and of religion, a calamitous succession of injuries given and

received, crimes which were our fault, and accidents which were no one's fault, have all contributed to make Englishmen ignorant of, and indifferent to, Ireland. It is true this rather explains than excuses their misconduct, but it is only fair to remember that ignorance rather than malice has been the cause of the long toleration of Ireland's wrongs. If, after recent revelations, England allows the old state of things to continue, she will not escape the reprobation of the civilized world.

Irish agitation has long been a by-word of reproach with large classes in this country, as something incurably perverse, factious, and unreasonable. Admitting for a moment that it has not seldom been all this, it is forgotten that antagonistic to it there has been, not an agitation, but a ceaseless action, a stedfast pressure of another kind, and from another source, which deserves even less complimentary epithets. While the fiery eloquence of O'Connell alarmed and disgusted Englishmen, who wanted only routine, peace, and good markets, a far more subtle, constant, and efficacious influence was at work to close their minds against every rational plea or grievance coming from Ireland. The Clergy of the Established Church, and the English proprietary of the country, by the very conditions of their existence, were, in a manner, compelled to misinform and mislead English public opinion as to the real state of matters in Ireland. To keep the conscience of England cold or even hostile to Ireland — the real Ireland ; Catholic, Celtic Ireland—was an essential pre-requisite to enable them to retain their position of ascendancy and power. How much self-seeking entered into O'Connell's agitation it may be difficult to decide ; there can be no question as to the motives of the Ascendancy party, who for years commanded the press and the ear of the middle and upper classes here. It was pointed out to England, with insinuating flattery, that her interest and her duty alike demanded that she should support them in their position of power and supremacy, that to listen to their accusers for a moment would be an act of folly and wickedness combined. England is great, we are told, by reason of her pure reformed faith, and of the glorious constitution which it is her happiness to possess. Are these precious, inestimable privileges to be risked or thrown away in deference to new-fangled notions of abstract justice to Ireland ? Is England to put a slight on the Bible and Gospel truth for the sake of conciliating idolatrous Romanists ? Is she to undermine the time-honoured customs and associations which have grown round her system of landed tenure, by countenancing revolutionary schemes in Ireland ? It is the thin end of the wedge which is thus being speciously inserted, and it will rend England after having rent Ireland. When you once begin doing what people call justice, there is no knowing where it will stop. It will be much better to leave Ireland alone. This language is even yet heard.

As regards Fenianism, it is the extreme stage of Irish discontent,—Irish disaffection to England grown into hatred and fury. It results from a multitude of causes. To say that any one thing is its cause would be erroneous, to hope that the removal of any one thing will dispel it is unreasonable. Let no one expect a sudden and magical diminution in the fierceness of Fenianism by reason of the decision of the House of Commons in favour of Mr. Gladstone's Resolutions. On the contrary, it is likely that vigorous Fenians will be irritated by such wisdom in their opponents. They will like the English Government none the better for competing with them for Irish loyalty and good-will. They know well they would not have a chance if the English Government honestly and heartily engaged in that competition. But, on the other hand—and this is a contingency to be feared—if we forthwith resume our wonted apathy and ignorance of Ireland and her wrongs, if we consider that, having with heroic courage knocked over one of the weakest shams that ever imposed upon mankind, we have discharged our debt to justice, then Fenians will rejoice, and head-centres be right glad. Then shall we have evidence of the futility, not indeed of doing justice to Ireland, but of continuing to support injustice.

I have not considered it incumbent on me to be profuse in offering remedies for Ireland's disorders. I consider it more important just at present to convince the English people that such disorders exist. I make no doubt whatever that when there is a unanimous will to satisfy Ireland a way will be found. But it is quite useless to prescribe medicines while half the physicians deny that anything ails the patient. Mr. Lowe never heard of a verified Irish grievance, and noble lord after noble lord declares that the country never was so settled, so improving, "slowly but steadily improving," as at this moment. While such opinions can be expressed, the object with reformers must be not to multiply schemes and panaceas, but to bring about a conviction in the public mind that a state of things exists in Ireland which urgently calls not only for remedies of some sort, but for our most determined resolution to discover them.

Irish grievances arise in connexion with the—

(1) Church Establishment,
(2) Land Tenure,
(3) Wounded Nationality.

Of these I shall treat in the above order.

I.—THE CHURCH.

THE long indictment of the Irish Church need not happily be repeated here. Reason, argument, statistics, ridicule, have long ago done their best and their worst upon that marvellous institution. Its continuance unto these days is a very pregnant and sobering fact, warning us how little power justice and truth have among men if unassisted by the stronger allies of interest and passion. On looking at it one thinks of the cynical saying that the very theorems of Euclid would be disputed if it were worth anybody's while to dispute them. It is so unjust, and at the same time so futile, that it is not easy to rid the mind of the conviction that it could never have been intended for anything but an elaborate and cruel practical joke. One, however, which has cost us dear. As the Dean of Cork [1] says, the world is weary of the subject, but not, perhaps,

---

[1] See article in the *Contemporary Review* for the month of March, perhaps the ablest defence that has appeared of the Irish Church Establishment ;—if there can be degrees in—nullity.

exactly for the reason which he supposes. We are weary of seeing the slain killed; we are weary of the lists and tabular statements of parishes containing "no Anglicans;" of others containing "under twenty Anglicans," of others under fifty, and so forth. It is our good fortune at this moment to be saved from the degradation of demonstrating over and over again the iniquity of injustice. A rapid and spontaneous ripening of public opinion has taken place on this topic, and declared with unmistakeable emphasis that the injustice shall no longer exist. It must be admitted that English opinion shirked the subject as long as it could. Everybody felt that the re-opening of it would be nearly certain to plunge the world into a cauldron of heated controversy, to expose every one to a devastating invasion of fanatics opposed to Romish error, of fanatics of the loaves and fishes side of the question, as represented in comfortable bishoprics and rich sinecures. Sober and thoughtful men shuddered and winced at the prospect. After all, who could hope that reason and justice would meet with a success in the future which they had ludicrously failed to attain in the past? Nothing could be added to the unanswerable arguments of Sydney Smith, Hallam, Macaulay, or, for the matter of that, of Lord Lytton and of Mr. Disraeli. What is the good of proving that black is black if people cannot see it for themselves ? "The eye sees only what the eye brings means of seeing." It is well perhaps that the public eye was trained to discriminate blackness from other shades in other directions than that of the Irish Church—to practise itself in tracing the lines of elementary justice in admiring foreign rebels against ecclesiastical oppression. However, no one could tell how far this training or any other had gone to enable the popular mind to take a fresh unbiassed view of the subject again. Above all, no one could tell how far the manifest spread among the cultivated classes of a secular tone of thought had imperceptibly honeycombed the old ramparts and bastions of Protestant orthodoxy. And now we see that it had gone further than could have been expected, that for the first time in our modern history the old No Popery appeal has been made in vain. It must be admitted that under the smooth surface of the last thirty years reflection has not been idle—an encouraging fact amid much which is discouraging.

As regards the so-called arguments in support of the Irish Church, they cannot be answered because they do not exist. This is one of the few cases, if it be not, as I believe, the only case having to do with the complicated phenomena of society and politics, in which all the arguments are really

as well as apparently on one side. Experience generally warns us to be on our guard against such cases.
Too clear a case is always more or less suspected.
It can hardly be doubted that the unparalleled injustice of the Irish Church has benefited that
institution through the impulse which prompts
men to disbelieve that all the reason and argument
can belong to one party in a dispute. And this im-
pression is never removed till we read the apologies
of the Establishment. The most scrupulously cau-
tious and sober attacks upon it always wear such
an incredible air of exaggeration, amounting almost
to caricature, that our judgment and impartiality
are disturbed and uneasy. But if any one wants to
make up his mind once for all on the subject, he has
only got to read a few charges by Irish bishops, or
pamphlets penned by Irish archdeacons. The real
use of attacks now on the Establishment is to
provoke those invaluable replies which at last have
convinced Englishmen, in spite of themselves, that
for once nothing is to be said on the other side.
Nothing else could have done it, not Smith's wit
and ridicule, not Macaulay's invective : none but
inmates of the stronghold could have so revealed
its weakness.

As a regular defence is impossible, recourse is
had to diversions. When Englishmen dwell on the

injustice of the Establishment, they are bidden to reflect on the perils they would incur by abolishing it. When they ask what is the use of pastors without flocks, of sheepfolds without sheep, they are told to consider the danger of countenancing a rival set of pastors whose flocks are multitudinous and whose pens are full. We are further told that whatever abstract justice may seem to demand, it is neither safe nor just to execute it. The Protestant garrison in Ireland embraces, we are assured, the only loyal subjects England retains in Ireland ; it would be at once a folly and a crime to alienate these our only friends, to degrade and injure them, the only allies we possess against hostile Papists and rebels. It is premature and sanguine to hope that this, the great Protestant bulwark argument, has lost all power because it is less triumphant than of yore. Doubtless it cannot carry matters with the high hand it once did, but it is still capable of much mischief, and is on every account worthy of attention.

When it is said that it is impolitic and unjust to alienate and injure friends for the doubtful prospect of conciliating foes, it is clear that the whole question turns upon who those friends are, and what are the conditions of their friendship. What is it we are expected to do to keep them friends ? Is it consistent with conscience, with reason ? It is

certain that friendship may be offered on terms
which no honest man or nation can accept. "You
stick to me and I will stick to you," is a bargain
which may be proposed to further objects the most
infamous. There are friends and friends, and some
are of a character from whom wise men pray to
be delivered. No one need have any difficulty in
finding friends, troops of friends, if no stipulations
are to be made as regards the terms of their friendship. The question now is, What does the friendship
of Irish Episcopalians cost us, not only in money,
but in self-respect, in justice, and in a clear conscience? And is their friendship or loyalty—if
it can only be had for the buying—worth its cost?
Is it not offered at a price outrageously too dear?
Can it help us towards peace and unity, or any one
of the objects of good government? Three hundred
years of disaffection and disunion give a sufficient
answer to the question.

Then, as regards the bulwark of Protestantism,
those amongst us who care about that can have
no difficulty in forming a judgment. This precious
bulwark is a wall of sand which every tide throws
down and washes away. The simple Protestant
public in this country has been over and over again
assured that the bulwark was in first-rate order;
that it was repelling its foes with victorious success;

that a little more sand would make it perfect and inexpugnable. Now positively for the last time was the Reformation going to prevail; now was Romish error about to fall prostrate before the advance of Gospel truth. The cruel census of 1861 dissipated those beautiful visions beyond hope. "After more than a quarter of a century of missionary labours within this district (the Dioceses of Tuam, Killala, and Achonry), the Anglicans have to show an absolute decrease of numbers from 21.765 in 1834, to 17,157 in 1861, or 4,608 individuals, being more than one fourth of their present total strength in their united dioceses." [1]

[1] *Freeman's Journal Church Commission,* 12th Report. Few are aware of the enormous sums annually devoted to the conversion of the Roman Catholics of Ireland, especially in the West. This money is disbursed by various Missionary Societies, which collect their funds chiefly from England and Scotland, and dispose of sums greater, it is computed, than the ordinary diocesan revenue of the sees in which they operate. One society alone enjoys an income averaging £24,000 per annum, and it is probable that since 1849 it has expended upwards of a quarter of a million sterling in this district. It is reasonable to suppose that the subscribers of these large sums would expect some return for their money. They were assured by several most exalted dignitaries of the Church that nothing could be more satisfactory. The Bishop of Winchester, in 1859, eighteen months before the Census, declared that he had seen "the churches crowded; meetings thronged to overflowing; and late comers, who could find no room, swarming like bees all round the building." Canon Wordsworth told them that "hundreds of thousands were flocking to the services of the Church." Archdeacon Stopford said that "ten thousands of Roman Catholics have openly cast off the religion of Rome, and are now amongst the most earnest and attentive

Or the unexceptionable testimony of Dr. Magee,
Dean of Cork, may be cited as to the probable
effects of abolishing the Establishment. " The result
would be," he says, " the handing over the half of
Ireland to the absolute mastery of the most Ultra-
montane priesthood in Europe ; the drying up of
the Anglican Church into Ulster and a few of the
larger towns of the other provinces." [1] If this
opinion be correct—and there is every reason to
suppose that the writer has both the opportunity
of knowing and the wish to speak the truth—
it certainly implies that the second Reformation
is still a long way off, and that the bulwark
hitherto has not done much for the money spent

members of the Church of England and Ireland." The Census showed
that in the Diocese of Tuam the whole Anglican population was 45·3
less than the number of converts represented to have left Rome. Two
of the four Connemara parishes have declined in the Anglican population 55 per cent. in ten years, while the three united Dioceses of Tuam,
Killala, and Achonry have exhibited the decrease mentioned in the
text.

Both religions lost during the famine and the subsequent emigration,—the Catholics far more than the Protestants, as belonging
mostly to the poorest class. The Anglicans also were reinforced by
.purchasers of land in the Encumbered Estates Court, and, last but not
least, by the large staff of imported missionaries. Consequently the
Protestants are now 3·37 per cent. of the whole population, whereas in
1834 they were 2·95, an apparent relative increase which must not
mislead. They are, after all, 4,608 less in number now than they were
then. See the above-cited *Freeman's Journal Church Commission,*
12th Report.

[1] *Contemporary Review,* March 1868.

upon it.[1] As far as statistics can elucidate such a point, they certainly go to prove that the Dean is right. In the Diocese of Cloyne there is a benefice named Nathlash, of which the net income is 207*l.* The gentleman who receives this sum yearly does so for giving ghostly comfort and advice to *one* Anglican parishioner. Nothing can seem more probable than, supposing the Establishment to be abolished, the Anglican Church, as far as this living is concerned, would dry up "either into Ulster" or elsewhere ; but it defies conception to see where would be the loss. Is it not dried up already ? One would like, at the cost of any

[1] Few persons have an idea of the sums thus expended merely on the material fabrics of the Establishment. Between 1834 and 1865 the following sums were devoted to the following purposes in the united Dioceses of Tuam, Killala, and Achonry :—

NO. OF CHURCHES.	HOW DEALT WITH.	COST.		
		£	*s.*	*d.*
4	Built.	4,419	18	6
8	Rebuilt.	9,549	19	8
10	Completed.	3,581	19	0
70	Repaired.	41,592	15	1
	Total	£59,144	12	3

It should be added that the Bishop and his clergy cost £27,756 a year, and that £10,187 was expended on the Bishop's palace in fifteen years. And these vast sums are spent for the dissemination of opinions which are not only condemned by the immense majority of Christians as heretical, but which clash in a growing discord with all the progressive tendencies of modern philosophy.

reasonable effort, to enter into the frame of mind which can contemplate such a contingency with horror and dismay. No one would wish the worthy and solitary Anglican in Nathlash to fall into evil ways, to forget his Protestant Bible, or to lose his orthodox abhorrence of Popish error; but is not his preservation from these dangers purchased at a perfectly monstrous cost, not only in money, but in national dignity and common sense? No one questions the importance of his or of anybody's spiritual welfare, but does it require that the State should step forward, in all its majesty, to endow and establish a Church for him, and for him alone, in order to further it? For it must be remembered that, although he is solitary in his religion, he is by no means solitary otherwise: in the parish of Nathlash he has 1,576 fellow-parishioners; but these the State entirely ignores. Its eagle eye can see him, and him only; its bountiful care can take thought only of him. Must he lose all religion if his spiritual pastor be withdrawn? would Protestantism receive an indelible wound if he did? Taking for granted that he is a loyal and attached friend of England by reason of the favour she shows him, would his enmity, if that favour were withheld, be a blow from which England could not be expected to recover? What would he do when we had outraged his feelings by abolishing the State Church which he has hitherto enjoyed? Would he declare war against us, or turn Fenian? It seems probable that, if the doctrines of Christianity have entered into the teaching given him by the nation for nothing, he will quietly read his Bible and say his prayers at home, without any violent anger at a great act of justice.

Again, we are threatened with another calamity if the State Church be abolished. The landed Protestant gentry, we are told, will leave the country at once under such a condition of things. "Such legislation," says the Dean of Cork, in solemn warning, "such legislation" (the abolition of the Establishment) "will surely bring with it its own Nemesis. It is not difficult to see even already of what kind that will be, in Ireland first, and next in England. In Ireland its results would be the rapid absorption by the Church of Rome of the poor and scattered Protestants of the South and West" (such as our friend at Nathlash for instance); "the departure, in consequence, of the Protestant country gentry, whose isolated position would then have become intolerable, and even dangerous." There is something very gloomy and sad in such a prospect, and all the more so that no one could have guessed there was any danger of its being realized. Imagine squires, broad-acred and broad-chested hunters of the fox, and pursuers of diverse kinds of small game, sitting down weary and sick at heart by reason of the fall of their beloved Church. Mirth and revelry and spontaneous joy would die away in Castle Rackrent when the spiritual welfare of its inmates was no longer paid for 'and looked after by the State. But, worse still, "their isolated position, become intolerable, and even dangerous," would force them into the frightful course of "departing" from Ireland. This reflection is positively harrowing. It makes one think of the Babylonish Captivity, the exiles of Siberia, and a series of melancholy occurrences. Painful as it may be, we shall have to endure their "departure." They will go, one may presume, into exile upon the banks of the Thames ·and the Seine, by whose waters they will weep less for themselves than for their unhappy native land. Then also, we may suppose, Irish absenteeism would become a reality instead of the fiction it has hitherto been.

I do not pretend that other pleas are not urged in defence of the Establishment. Some insist that it deserves support as it teaches the "truth as it is in Jesus," which it is the duty of the State to further by all available means. Others urge that they have got their revenues, and that they mean to keep them if they can—a good downright practical view of the subject. Others tell us that the State can give, but cannot take away. It refreshes one's faith in the progress of the human mind to observe that the bulk of the public has grown deaf to the charm of these arguments, charm they never so wisely. It is to be hoped that the nation will proceed calmly but sternly to a great act of long-deferred justice, perfectly regardless, as Mr. Carlyle expresses it, of the screamings and lamentations of doleful creatures. At the same time too much must not be expected from one act of justice, when many are due. Disappointment must not be felt if an instalment does not produce the effects which commonly result from paying the full sum. In a word, it must not be supposed that doing what is right in one direction will exonerate us from doing the same in others, which are equally urgent. We must not forget that settling the Church question is only a preliminary to settling the more vital one concerning the land.

II.—THE LAND.

THE remarkable consensus of opinion which has been manifested with regard to the inauguration of religious equality in Ireland is strikingly absent with reference to the far deeper and more vital question of the Tenure of Land in that country. Theologians and ecclesiastics have, so to speak, had their day; they can look to little beyond fair and equal justice, while any favouritism towards them on the part of the State is becoming daily more and more discredited. But landlordism is still a mighty power, upon which thousands cast reverent eyes. A bishop lamenting over his invaded privileges is not unfrequently more ridiculed than condoled with. But a landlord protesting, however unnecessarily, against interference with the sacred right of property, is still felt to be a solemn object, suggestive of grave and anxious meditation. Many new ideas will have to be acquired, and many old ones laid aside, before a clearness with reference to the Land question at all equal to that which we have seen concerning the Established Church is likely to be generally attained.

Nothing can exceed the confusion and obscurity in which the whole subject is involved, and, so to speak, all but buried. So anxious is each disputant to have his say, that no one thinks of taking heed of what is said by his neighbour. It is a fierce conflict waged in the night. The adversaries do not even use the same language. When one speaks of improvements and the welfare of the country, he means something very different from what an opponent means who uses the same words. To join false issues is all but universal; to assert vehemently what was never denied, to demonstrate elaborately what has never been called in question, is a sort of rule of the game in this controversy. There is not even anything like agreement as to what are the ends and objects of the strife. While one set of disputants tells us that the Land question in Ireland is precisely the most urgent and important which can possibly be entertained, another set tells us with equal confidence that there is no Land question at all, and the whole affair is a bubble blown up by interested agitators. Perhaps the best mode of commencing this inquiry will be to ascertain these points first. Is there a Land question? and, if so, In what does it consist?

IS THERE A LAND QUESTION ? It is evident that this question may be answered in twenty ways, according to the bias and position of the respondent. If, before the abolition of the slave-trade, a planter had been asked whether there was a Nigger Question, in the sense of the abolitionist, he would have answered that decidedly there was not. That is to say, he would not have denied that slavery existed; he would have denied that it was a thing to be complained of. In a similar spirit the landlords of the present day deny that there is a Land question in Ireland. They do not, of course, deny that dissatisfaction or rather "agitation" exists; they deny that it has any meaning or reason in it. "What," asked Lord Clanricarde recently in the House of Lords, "what was the condition of Ireland now ? There never was a time when it was less necessary to take extraordinary and novel action upon this subject than at present. The condition of neither landlords nor tenants presented any extraordinary difficulty." And his lordship proceeds to throw the blame of the attention which has been directed to the subject upon the judges. Further on he said: "There was no occasion for a revolution. This year rents had been easily collected and most cheerfully paid in Ireland. Profits had been made by the farmers, and this year the landlords had had

less trouble than perhaps at any former period."
(*Times,* Feb. 25, 1868.) And Lord Dufferin holds
language which points to the same conclusion. He
declares that fixity of tenure would not materially
have impeded the exodus after the potato famine,
which must mean that Irish holders would have
been as unsettled and as uncomfortable with fixity
of tenure as they have been without it.[1] Lord Rosse
says : "At present things are steadily improving."
And an "Irish Peer," who has written a noteworthy
pamphlet on the "Irish Difficulty," says, that if
they are only preserved from "an agrarian law,
subverting the foundations of all landed property"
—and the compulsory granting of leases he would
consider to be such a subversion—"Irish agriculture will soon become assimilated to that of England."[2] Now all these utterances obviously mean
only this, that the Irish proprietors are, on the
whole, satisfied with the actual state of things.
The fact is not surprising, and has never been called
in question. People generally are content with
what they deliberately and intentionally bring
about.

Fortunately the condition and progress of a

[1] "Irish Emigration and Tenure of Land in Ireland." Willis and
Sotheran, 1867.
[2] "The Irish Difficulty," by an Irish Peer, p. 60. Hodges and
Smith, Dublin.

country are not now a matter of guess-work and individual opinion. However satisfactory the tenure of land in Ireland may be to the landlords, we are not reduced to abiding by their estimate. Whether things are steadily improving or not from Lord Rosse's point of view, from an economical point of view they are doing precisely the reverse. Without reference to the vexed questions between proprietors and occupiers, without an allusion to tenant-right or landlord-wrong, Ireland is a far less productive country than it was formerly, even during the years which it is the fashion to look back upon with horror, viz. those preceding and following the famine. A few statistics taken from Thom's Almanack, which are based on returns made to Parliament, and, I believe, of unimpeached accuracy, are here indispensable. We find that—

In 1847 the number of acres under wheat was 743,871. In 1866 it was 299,190.

In 1847 the number of acres under oats was 2,200,870. In 1866 it was 1,699,695.

In 1847 the number of acres under barley was 345,070. In 1866 it was 160,314.

In 1847 the number of acres under beans was 23,768. In 1850 it was 62,590. But in 1866 it had fallen to 14,804.

Or take the estimated produce :—

In 1847 the wheat crop amounted to 2,926,733 quarters. In 1866 it had fallen to 805,710.

The oats had fallen from 11,521,606 to 7,284,835 quarters within the same period.

The barley, bere, and rye had fallen from 1,716,139 to 685,717 quarters.

Taken altogether the corn crops in 1847 were spread over 3,813,579 acres. In 1866 they had shrunk to 2,173,433.

It must be admitted that these are startling figures. They indicate an extraordinary diminution of production during the most productive era the world has ever known. It looks odd to be told, in the presence of such facts, that things are steadily improving. It is requisite to add that there is a set-off against this decrease in the increase under the heads of meadow and clover, live-stock, flax, and potatoes. But even the meadow and clover last year were not as productive by upwards of 300,000 tons as they were in 1860 ; the cattle are not as numerous now by 100,000 head as they were in 1859 ; while the immense development of the flax culture and industry was a temporary and artificial growth stimulated by the dearth of cotton during the American Civil War.[1]

[1] Thom's Almanack for 1868. Statistics, pp. 779, 785. I append,

It thus appears that economically at least there is a very serious Land question in Ireland.

And if we regard the matter socially and politically it is not better, but worse. Discontent and

on Mr. Butt's authority, the following evidence of decrease in Irish manufactures :—

"In 1800 there were engaged in the woollen manufacture 91 master manufacturers ; in 1840 these were reduced to 12; in 1864 to 8.

"In 1800 the hands employed were 4,038 ; in 1841 these were reduced to 682.

"In 1800 there were in the town of Roscrea in Tipperary 900 persons supported by the woollen factories ; at present there are none.

"In 1800 the manufacture of flannel in the county of Wicklow employed 1,000 looms ; at present in all that county there is not 1.

"In 1800 there were 30 master wool-combers in Dublin ; in 1835 they were reduced to 5.

"In 1800, in Kilkenny, a blanket manufactory existed which gave employment to 3,000 operatives ; in 1841 these were reduced to 925.

"In 1800 there were 1,491 persons employed in the city of Dublin in stuff serge manufacture ; in 1834 they were reduced to 131.

"In 1800, 720 operatives were employed in the carpet manufacture under 13 masters ; in 1841 there was but 1 carpet maker."—*The Irish People and the Irish Land,* by Isaac Butt.

We may add to these figures the following, taken from the " Statesman's Year Book for 1868 : "—

All Ireland has 9 cotton factories ; Lanark alone in Scotland has 83 cotton factories.

2,734 Irishmen are engaged in manufacturing cotton; 41,273 Scotchmen are occupied with the same business.

But this last fact admits of another comparison. In *all* the factories of all Ireland, the male and female hands employed number 37,872. Thus the cotton factories *alone* of Scotland exceed in the number of their operatives the total of the factories of Ireland by upwards of 3,000 hands.

Or compare the cotton trade of Scotland with the linen trade of Ireland ;

Scotland has 138 cotton factories.
Ireland has 100 flax factories.

disaffection towards the established order of things have notoriously reached an alarming pitch in that country. To say that the farmers are not the Fenians is futile. The Fenians are the fighting division of Irish disaffection. The English army at Waterloo was not the English nation, but it represented the English nation; the Fenians are not the Irish nation, but they represent the large element in it which is hostile and fierce against English rule.[1] Their ranks are recruited from many classes, the farmer class included, but their moral strength and capital consist in the sympathy and

---

Yet flax is Ireland's specialty, and the population of Ireland is very nearly double that of Scotland.

To conclude this long note :—

In January 1846 there were 19,883 fishing-vessels, employing 93,073 men and boys ; in 1866 the numbers respectively were 9,444 vessels and 40,663 men and boys ; thus making a decrease of 10,439 vessels, and 52,410 men and boys, engaged in that occupation in 21 years.

[1] This fact is persistently denied by the upper class in Ireland, and their advocates in the English press. But the following testimony from Mr. Marcus Keane may probably be considered sufficient to outweigh a good deal of contrary evidence. Mr. Keane is, as he says, land agent of several large estates—among others of that of the Marquis of Conyngham—and a land proprietor himself. He says : "The strength of Fenianism lies in the sympathy which it receives from a large majority of the tenant class. As a mere conspiracy Fenianism is not very formidable, but as a principle pervading the Irish nation—active in the minds of multitudes who never thought of becoming avowed Fenians—I look upon it as more serious than I can easily find words to express."—*Letter addressed to Col. Vandeleur, M.P., on the Irish Land Question,* by Marcus Keane.

encouragement they receive from nearly all who are not landlords and clergymen of the Established Church. Nothing is easier than to say that this disaffection is unreasonable, perverse, and wicked. Persons against whom such complaints are made always consider disaffection perverse, from the Kaiser on his throne to the fish-wife skinning the eels and cursing them for not being quiet. The charge is that the position of the Irish tenantry has gradually become absolutely intolerable, that the people are leaving the country rather than endure it any longer, and that they carry away with them hearts swelling with the most savage animosity against the laws and the country which in their minds are the cause of their sufferings.

In what does the Land Question consist? I wish, with as little of hypothesis or of disputable matter as possible, to answer this question by a statement of such facts as are admitted by all, or nearly all, parties. The interpretation of these facts will come afterwards.

(1) The great mass of the Irish tenantry have no better title to their holdings than the will of their landlords.[1]

---

[1] This paragraph and the next are taken literally from the last-cited letter of Mr. M. Keane ; it would be impossible to adduce weightier authority.

(2) The rentals of Ireland are steadily following the improvements of the tenants. Some landlords suffer a considerable margin to exist between the actual value and the rent paid, while others lose no opportunity of forcing the rents to the highest amount that circumstances permit.

(3) This state of things is one absolutely and entirely new. The granting of leases was the general custom in the last century, and continued for some time into this.

(4) The agriculturists of Ireland never had such a feeble and precarious hold upon the land they cultivate as they have now. It appears certain that this precariousness of tenure has no parallel or equal in the world. It is peculiar to Ireland, and new even there.

(5) It is, however, an object which the all but unanimous efforts of - the landlords are directed to bring about. It is an object which they avowedly pursue both for their own interests and the interests, as they allege, of agricultural improvement.

(6) They have by their persevering and combined efforts brought this precariousness of tenure very nearly to a degree of completeness.

(7) Their control over their tenants is practically absolute. They can and do enact bye-laws on their

estates which place the tenant for practical purposes in a state of serfdom. By their rules marriage has been known to be forbidden without the licence of the agent; while one of the most general of these bye-laws is that which forbids the harbouring of any, except the tenant's immediate family, in his house.[1]

(8) These powers are exercised by means of a summary ejectment code which is unknown to the English law, and gives extraordinary facilities of ejectment to the Irish landlord.

(9) And these powers, conferred by the law, are increased by skill in the management of estates. A tenancy from year to year is reduced to an actual

---

[1] "I could tell of another estate on which the landlord's agent has laid down the rule that under no circumstances shall two families be permitted to live in the same house." "An aged widow invited her daughter, who had lost her husband, to take share of her house. For this crime, although occupying a respectable position, the mother of a Roman Catholic priest, she is actually evicted from a farm where she had lived for nearly fifty years."—*Plea for the Celtic Race*, p. 27, by Isaac Butt. Mr. Butt vouches for this on his own personal knowledge.

"The tenancy is determinable by a month's notice or the death of the tenant, and further, according to some of their rules and conditions, the tenant cannot marry or procure the marriage of his son or daughter without the landlord's or the agent's permission. Moreover, he cannot entertain, even for a night, not merely the stranger who asks his hospitality, but even his nearest relative and friend." Quoted by Mr. Butt, *loco citato*, from an address delivered before the Legal and Historical Society, by their president, Mr. C. Molloy. The story of the "homeless boy," which illustrates the same system, is too long for a note, and is placed in Appendix A.

tenancy at will by the contrivance of an annual notice to quit, or by an agreement binding the tenant under a heavy penalty to give up possession whenever he is asked.[1] It is stated that a receipt for rent on some estates is never given without a printed notice to quit on the back of it.[2]

[1] I take this statement from Mr. Butt, who it may be presumed knows the law on this matter (" The Irish People and the Irish Land," p. 244).

Mr. Thos. de Moleyns, Q.C., in his work. " The Landowner's and Agent's Practical Guide," remarks :—" The Sheriff may execute any *habere* or civil bill decree for possession, without removing any under-tenant or occupier who shall at the time of such execution sign with his name or mark an attornment or acknowledgment of title according to forms Nos. 6 or 7 in the Schedule A." (This is the pith of the form referred to : We, whose names are hereunder subscribed, hereby acknow-ledge that we respectively occupy the lands by the licence and at the will of the said A. B. . . . and that we will *when required by the said A. B* deliver up to the said A. B. the possession of the said lands, &c. &c.) " The 71st Section of the Landlord and Tenant Act now regulates the conditions, which appear to be rather arbitrary, of redemption in both Courts. The Court is to hear the application and give such relief in a summary way as a Court of Equity might have formerly done, and may award restitution to the tenant or refuse his application. It is thus left to the discretion of the Judge or Chairman to impose such terms as he may think reasonable."

[2] I have been told this by most respectable persons who knew it to be a fact. Lord Dufferin says : " To serve an ejectment is very often the only way of inducing a dilatory tenant to pay up an arrear of rent ; in which case it bears the same relation to an eviction as a lawyer's letter to an action at law. On my own estate, dozens of ejectments have been served for one eviction that has taken place, and the more indulgent the landlord, the more disposed will some of his tenants be to wait for this proof of his patience being exhausted,"—an observation which testifies to a peculiar state of things, and hardly agrees with the very good understanding which Lord Dufferin declares elsewhere to exist between landlords and their tenants.

(10) It is not pretended that good landlords do
not exist, who take an enlarged view of their duties,
and display a wise generosity in their dealings with
their tenants; but it is an accepted principle in
politics not to trust the public welfare to the exceptional virtue of individuals. Injustice, oppression,
and bad government could not exist if this were safe
to do. Even in the crucial case of slavery it is
unquestionable that good masters were to be found
whose conscience was a law unto themselves. The
Southern planters were not all Legrees; far from
it. But the system admitted of Legrees, and was
condemned by all good men in consequence. Landlordism in Ireland presents on a diminished scale a
parallel condition of things. One wicked unscrupulous landlord can work a mischief which ten good
ones would not suffice to counteract, even if there
were always ten good ones to neutralize one bad
one, which would be a rather extravagant supposition. The system gives powers which, human nature
being what it is, are sure to be abused by a certain
number at any given moment; and, as no one who
lives under it can have any guarantee that he will
not be subject to one of them, the uneasiness and
distrust are universal.

Such in rude outline are the chief heads of tenant-
wrong in Ireland. It must, I think, be admitted

that, however such a state of affairs is to be explained, or however it has been brought to pass, it is one suggestive of grave and even of anxious thought. Everybody can judge for himself whether uncertainty, hopeless insecurity concerning the future, is not one of the most painful and paralysing sentiments which can afflict the mind. In this case it is a sentiment which is shared by the great bulk of those who live by labour—by those who are employed upon the chief industry of the country. Any diminution of enterprise or of production appears possible or probable under such a system. To live always under the favour or caprice of an agent or landlord, who can terminate your trade and industry whenever he thinks fit, can lead but to one result, —the sullen discontent and apathy of the persons so situated.

We now come to the interpretation to be put upon these facts by the advocates of the landlords and tenants respectively.

The former, after they have referred to the lofty argument of their right to do as they like with their own, plead that they have been driven into adopting the present system by considerations of public duty no less than of private interest. Nothing less stern than the measures they now adopt can save Ireland from becoming a pauper warren, as it was before the famine. Leases invariably lead to subletting and subdividing of farms ; subdivision again leads to the ruin of agriculture. Irish tenants cannot be trusted with leases.[1] The only use they put one to is first to ruin themselves, and then their landlord. Page after page of Lord Dufferin's work on the land tenure of Ireland is devoted to prove this point by means of extracts from the Report of the Devon Commission. A land agent, who has written a clever pamphlet in answer to Mr. Butt's "Plea for the Celtic Race," declares that the tenants will invariably neglect the most elementary principles of farming. The landlord's agent is ceaselessly active in keeping them up to their work. It is not too much to say that something like idiocy is charged against the agriculturists of Ireland by the owners of the soil.[2] They will not or cannot cul-

---

[1] To prove this thesis is the practical object of Lord Dufferin's book, " Irish Emigration and the Tenure of Land in Ireland." It is difficult to get a clear conception of what Lord Dufferin really thinks on this question of leases. He frequently admits that leases are highly important, even necessary, to good agriculture. At the same time he argues strenuously to prove that it is mere madness to give Irish tenants leases ; that "security of tenure, instead of stimulating the industry of the occupier, too often acts as a premium on idleness, and the difficulties of preventing the subdivision and subletting of leased lands are almost insurmountable."—*Irish Emigration*, p. 266.

[2] " Few who have not tried it can have any idea of the difficulty of getting the ordinary tenants to maintain improvements made by the landlord without any expense to the tenant, and solely for his

tivate the land in a proper manner, and they will subdivide it to a degree which renders good farming impossible. Hence the policy of not granting leases. They are thus held well in hand. Their sins of omission and commission are swiftly discovered and corrected; and if with all this care they will not mend, the facilities for ejectment afford the landlord a ready means of replacing them by more docile subjects. Agricultural improvement demands that the landlord should be armed with these powers. "One of the landlord's most important duties," says Lord Dufferin, "is that of insuring the consummate cultivation of his estate." To effect this end, it is frequently his stern but inevitable duty to improve the actual cultivators off the face of it. The prosperity of Ireland demands that the consolidation of small farms now going on shall be continued, and this can be accomplished only by an elimination of the still superfluous population,

benefit. For instance, I do not think of a single case of a watercourse deepened by a landlord (generally at a considerable expense), that I have not to inspect it continually to endeavour to induce them to keep it clear, by perhaps a couple of hours' work in clearing of weeds or deposit, from the effect of which the whole benefit is neutralized, and very often finding them literally dammed across by an embankment or large stones, for the purpose of making an easy way of crossing to the other side. The real fact being that the majority of small farmers and cottiers require to be watched and coaxed like children, to do what they admit to be for their own good." —*A Demurrer to Mr. Butt's Plea*, p. 37, by an Irish Land Agent.

who, as there is no other industry to receive them, will have to emigrate, to their own immense advantage, and of those who remain behind, whatever interested agitators may say to exacerbate their minds at an inevitable necessity.

This defence of the policy of the landlords—which, I hope, I shall not be accused of understating—is well worthy of consideration. In the first place, no impartial inquirer will deny that in many of the allegations there is much truth. It still remains to be seen how far it is to the point. It might all be true, and yet not in the least excuse the present policy of the landlords. For what is the gist of the charge against the tenants? Is it not that they are shiftless, improvident, and idle when they can be? In other words, that they lack those qualities of energetic independence which are the strength of states? And what is the remedy? What is the principle adopted to meet this condition of things? The answer is, that the principle is that of the pedant who declared he would never go into the water again till he had learned to swim. The Irish tenant is improvident; he shall, therefore, have no opportunity of exercising forecast and prudence. His readiness to undergo prolonged exertion is not always as prompt as it might be; therefore the inducement to endure sustained labour, the sweet rewards of continued toil contained in the certainty of reaping when he has sown, of enjoying the fruits when he has planted the seed, are to be withheld from him. These inducements are for thrifty Scotchmen and Englishmen, not for careless improvident Irishmen.

Suppose, for argument's sake, that the Irish tenant has all the demerits and defects which the literary landlords, who are now attacking him, lay to his charge. What is the inference? Is it not this, that he, like all of us, wants improving? that neither his intellect, nor conscience, nor energy, are what it is highly desirable they should be? If he lacks thrift and industry and intelligence, how are these virtues to be imparted to him? By treating him like a child or a serf, or by treating him like a free man? Let it be admitted that, coming as he does of a race which has been debilitated and crushed for ages, he does by no means fly with an irrepressible alacrity to avail himself of every opportunity that offers to push his remote and permanent interests; let it be granted that Lord Dufferin's report is true, and that if a tract of land strikes you as very ill-cultivated, you generally find that it is let on lease. It would be strange if such were not the case. Irish tenants have faults peculiar to them as a class, as other classes have. To suppose

that any individual among them will instantly free
himself from those faults the moment circumstances
begin to permit him to do so,—to expect that he
will at once show far-sighted wisdom the moment
the narrowest opportunity offers,—is to suppose that
he is endowed with qualities almost superhuman. He
lives by the hypothesis in the midst of a thriftless,
apathetic population. Most of his neighbours have
no inducement to be anything else but apathetic.
He gets or inherits a lease, and wonder is forthwith
expressed that all the habits which have been cultivated in him and his ancestors, and are general
among his compeers, do not drop from him like a
garment the moment, were he all-wise, they should
so fall. Is the prompt seizure and employment of
opportunities so universal a characteristic of human
nature, that we have reason to marvel at its absence
in the Irish tenant? Do lawyers invariably expand
into statesmen the moment they get into Parliament? Do martinets become as a rule great
generals the instant they assume great commands?
Nothing can be more absurd than the whole argument. The fact is, that Irish tenants are not
thrifty, far-sighted, energetic, like Scotch, Swiss, or
Belgian farmers ; and the reason of that fact is,
that there is nothing in their position to make them
so, but much to make them the reverse. When

such men do get, under a lease, a chance of displaying virtues they never had the opportunity of using or acquiring before, is that conclusive against them ? It is the peculiar iniquity of the present system of things that it appears to mark independence and self-help as odious vices which must at all risks be suppressed. When a man is fined for energy, it is not wonderful if he becomes slothful.[1] When a man does not know where he will be in a year's time—whether he will be left unmolested on his farm, or a wandering outcast—it is no marvel that deep-laid plans for the future are not often in his thoughts. He literally would be a fool to harbour them. He may be the most thrifty and enterprising of mortals, but the fatal want of security utterly forbids him to develop those qualities. The system sweeps over the land, mowing down the high and the low to the same level. Apathy, sullenness, and incompetence are seen to be as useful and fashionable as their contraries. A bad and feeble tone is the result throughout the class. We all know how a college, a regiment, a public office, a constituency may

[1] One of the most distinguished of the scientific men of Ireland recently told me the following anecdote :—Seeing a farmer whom he knew to be not without means clad in the most shabby and tattered garments, he asked him the reason. "Sure," said the other, " the last new coat cost me 2s. 6d. an acre more rent."

acquire a depreciated *morale*, which will defy all attempts at improvement from within, and the presence of public opinion from without, for years. The present condition of the House of Lords offers a parallel which is worthy of consideration. What is the complaint daily waxing louder against that assembly? That it does nothing; that it will not do what it still could; that it is listless and apathetic to a degree that renders the development of a statesman within it all but an impossibility. Every superior man in it has been trained in "another place." Why is this? Because the rewards of political energy and toil have departed from the House of Lords. The Lords were energetic enough when they had something to gain or lose by their energy. The Irish tenants, when they get to America or the Colonies, are also energetic when it is worth their while. Now, they have no more inducement to be zealous agriculturists than the Lords have to be zealous debaters.

But all through this discussion I have been proceeding on a supposition which I said was only admitted provisionally and for the sake of argument. It is quite certain that, even under the present system, many tenants improve—"they must improve," as Mr. Marcus Keane says, "in order to live comfortably." The large sums also deposited in the savings-banks show that they are thrifty and provident. And this takes place all the time that the working bees are constantly despoiled of their honey as fast as it is made ; and if they are not actually despoiled, they have no security that in a near future they will not be, as the good landlord under whom they happen to live may die or sell his property, and thus expose them to an unscrupulous successor.[1]

[1] The following appeal was heard at the last Spring Assizes at Mayo before Mr. Justice Keogh :—

THE LAW LIFE ASSURANCE COMPANY *v.* M‘GIRR.

"This was an appeal from a decree in ejectment obtained by the company in the court below. It appeared that the defendant in the year 1852 took a farm, being a portion of the extensive estates of the company in this county, at a rent of 44*l.*, the Ordnance valuation being 40*l.* When his first lease was at an end, the company raised the rent to 54*l.*, and the defendant was willing to pay this rent if the company would consent to build the necessary fences on the land ; and this not having been done, the defendant, for the purpose of bringing the matter before the Board of Directors, served their land agent with a notice of surrender. This had the desired effect, and a sum of between 70*l.* and 90*l.* was expended in fencing, and a percentage for this outlay added to his rent. He then signed a three years' lease, which having expired, he continued a tenant from year to year ; and as the land was only partially fenced, he asked the company either to complete the fencing, or, if they gave him the land at a fair rent, he would expend 200*l.* in fencing and draining. The offer was not acceded to, and to induce the company to move in the matter the defendant again served a notice of surrender. This, however, had a contrary effect, for, on the expiration of the notice of surrender, the Law Life Company brought an ejectment and obtained a decree. His lordship, in giving judgment, said he was bound to affirm the decree with costs ; but it was another of the many instances of the way in which property was managed in this country. Here was a great

When a large and influential body of men are seen pursuing with remarkable unanimity a particular line of conduct, which leads to general and important results, it is reasonable to conclude that they are actuated thereto by strong and adequate motives. It is also probable, from well-known potency of class selfishness, that these motives are not of a kind which would allow of an undisguised publicity. To cloak such unpresentable motives under the pretence of a generous solicitude for the common good is an expedient which experience

---

English company resident in London, having extensive estates in this county and in the county of Galway, and whose system, it appeared, was to let their lands to tenants from year to year. In this case they had a tenant who it was admitted was a man with means, who had always paid his rent up to last November ; and when last December he was served with his ejectment, he was also served with a civil bill for the November rent, and which he at once paid. It was plain from the correspondence in the case that the defendant was a person of intelligence and education. He, by his letters, asks this great company to do that which every English landlord does—to fence the farm, or to put him in a position to expend his own money in doing so, and their answer to that is an ejectment. Could such a thing as this happen with a resident landlord, with whom the tenant could have a personal interview ? but dealing with this company, it was highly improbable that any of their tenants would ever see a landlord in the flesh, as this great corporation were not resident here, never came here, or discharged those duties which the owners of property owed it to the country to discharge. He, however, sat there to administer the law, and he should affirm the decree, not only with the costs incident to it, but with the additional sum of 10s. 6d. demanded by the company as the travelling expenses of their own bailiffs, who came to prove the case."

See also Appendix B.

tells us is not seldom resorted to. In this case of the land tenure of Ireland we have seen that an elevated and patriotic regard for the welfare of agriculture and the nation at large is pleaded in defence of the policy pursued. The evidence should be very strong on this point, inasmuch as the presumption would certainly lie the other way,—would irresistibly lead to the conclusion that a very unscrupulous class interest was being followed. A system which satisfies only 8,000 individuals of a population considerably over five millions, which drives these millions into a state of chronic anger or despair, requires very ample and conclusive vindication to get it accepted by impartial men. Lord Dufferin indeed asserts that nothing but a solemn conviction of its importance to the public welfare induces him and others of his class to adopt it. It is highly necessary that this position should be examined.

The argument stated shortly is this. Good husbandry is impossible with the condition of things which, till recently, existed in Ireland. Irish tenants, when left to themselves, and indulged with leases, produced results which culminated in the great famine, execrable agriculture, and a pauper population. To prevent a recurrence of such a calamity, say the landlords, is now our determined intention. Noble, disinterested feelings actuate us in this course. Competition, it is well known, sends up rents. We are traders in land, and we at least should not have reason to complain of the multitude of our customers.[1] We have no objection to *la petite culture* which grew up under the old system of leases, as it was found peculiarly advantageous to landlords. We now object to it, simply because we conscientiously believe it is a bad system.[2] It is true, a considerable emigration is necessary for the completion of our plans. But that is an evil or a good to which all mankind at one period or another have been exposed. Indeed, we do not wish for emigration ourselves. We should be glad if the people would turn to other employment. We do not necessarily say that they need go away from Ireland, but they certainly shall go away from our farms. Agricultural improvement demands that. Two men on an English farm do as much work as four men do on an Irish farm. Ireland is in one of those transitional states which are always full of pain. A change is taking place in Irish agriculture which "resembles the revolution which overturned the manufacturing system of England on the introduction of the power-loom." We are not to be compelled to retain an unprofitable or exploded

---

[1] Lord Dufferin, "Irish Emigration," p. 24.
[2] Lord Dufferin, answer to Mr. Mill, p. 23.

system of husbandry, and it is wicked to revile us because we are doing the best thing for the country and the people.[1]

Now the first point in this argument to be noticed is, that the word "improvement" is used ambiguously. It is a word which, like liberty, is susceptible of varying definitions. Improving the husbandry of Ireland does not necessarily bring along with it improvement in the condition of the husbandmen of Ireland. If, in consequence of improved husbandry, one out of every two husbandmen is to be thrown out of employment, it is clear that great misery must be the result. It is all very well to say that the unemployed man can do something else; practically, he cannot; he must either starve or emigrate. "So much the better for him," say the landlords. And this might be admitted, if the remaining husbandman left behind were at once placed in a settled position of content and comfort in consequence. But we know he is not. We know he is placed in a position of greater insecurity and discomfort than ever he was before. We know that he has not a fraction of a guarantee that he will not have, at a few months' notice, to follow his brother into exile. Now to tell us that scientific agriculture is going to thrive on this

[1] "Irish Emigration," p. 197.

E

condition of things becoming general is simply to mistake the means for the end—to declare that men were made for farming, not that farming was invented for the sake of men. What does good farming exist for, if it be not to produce an increased supply of food for more men? Increased production is, no doubt, an excellent thing, but in our zealous pursuit of it we are not permitted to forget the human agencies by which it is brought about. All capitalists, whether manufacturers, landowners, or slave-owners, are dreadfully prone to overlook this important truth. But it is an oversight which the conscience of mankind is growing yearly less disposed to allow. If the condition of the producers is not to count at all, there is no valid argument against slavery in plantations. But the tendency is to insist that production shall not go on at the cost of sacrificing the producer. This principle is at the root of all the disputes and difficulties in the great debate between capital and labour. The slaves in Jamaica were far more productive before emancipation than they are now. But the conscience of England said and says, That may be, but we will not stand slavery all the same. And, nauseous as the principle may be to the *fruges consumere nati* of all orders, it is quite certain to prevail.[1]

_____
[1] It is quite unnecessary to point out that the pretext of improved

But further, although the economizing of labour by means of improved methods and machinery often tells heavily on the contemporary artisans who are displaced by the change, yet in the long run their class does not suffer, but much the reverse. The power-loom was doubtless a blow to the hand-weavers, but the consequent expansion of the cotton business compensated the operative class a hundred-fold. Lord Dufferin is fond of comparing land-owners to traders; they are traders in land, he says. Can he promise agricultural class compensation of increased employment similar to what the Lancashire millowners have been able to offer? Will the land trade expand in Ireland as the cotton trade did in Blackburn, Preston, and Manchester? He proposes to make it not only stationary but retrograde, so far as concerns the number of hands employed. And Lord Clanricarde recently in the House of Lords held language of similar import. Speaking of Belgian agriculture with the contempt it appears to deserve, in his opinion, he asked his audience: "In passing through Belgium, did their lordships see steam ploughs and steam thrashing-machines on the farms? No! But they saw women labouring in the fields, and doing work which in

agriculture and increased production is merely a pretext, and has no foundation in fact.

this country was done by machinery." (*Times*, Feb.
25, 1868.) It is clear that in the eyes of these
noblemen the most objectionable sight in a land-
scape are the human beings who till the land of it.
Reduce them as much as possible, and it will be
well with you : replace them by steam machinery,
and it will be better still. The unattainable but
ravishing ideal of this system would be to get the
land cultivated by one colossal steam-engine, tended
by a company of stokers. "Consummate cultivation" would then be obtained, without the need of
an agrarian class, who are now a necessary evil, but
who also are often troublesome and in the way. As
the world was made for landowners and rich people,
such an arrangement would lead to everything that
could be desired. It is possible, on the other hand,
that this beatific vision may not prove so fascinating
to the "masses." At any rate, if the landlords are
really bent on becoming manufacturers, and nothing
else, of corn, meat, and grain crops, let the fact be
known, and let us have as speedily as possible legislation which will do for the labourers and tenants
what the "Factory Acts" have done for the operatives.

But we have not yet done justice to the magnanimous and conscientious motives which lead
landlords to withhold leases.

The truth of the matter is this : the famine gave the landlords such a fright, that they have not yet recovered from it. Partly by their own apathy and carelessness, partly by their grasping at the nearest means to increase their political influence, and partly by the operation of other causes, the tenantry of Ireland before the year 1846 were mostly paupers. Even before that fatal year the danger was sighted. "The evil (of pauper tenants) grows to an extent that threatens the annihilation of the landlord's income," said the Devon Commissioners. Then came the famine, which, while it killed or exiled the tenants, gave also a heavy blow to the landlords. The shock sobered them at once. They perceived that *laissez faire* may be carried too far. They resolved that nothing of the kind should ever occur again. I do not suppose that they ever dreamed that any other course was open to them than the one they took, and it may be admitted that it did not exceed the ordinary measure of class-selfishness when left to itself. They evicted the pauper tenants, and made their successors tenants-at-will. It is not necessary to deny the public spirit and unselfishness of such a policy, but it is necessary to remark that it exactly coincided with their pecuniary interests, their privileges, and their pride. First of all, tenants became more completely exposed to coercion than ever before; the increased power over them was often useful at election times. But secondly, "an evil which threatened the annihilation of the landlord's income" was removed a good way off, if not utterly destroyed. Pauper warrens were not permitted to form again. This precaution was doubly necessary, in consequence of the new Poor-law which had been introduced a short time previously. Indeed, a small episode in the history of that important measure is worthy of being recalled, as it is highly illustrative of landlord legislation. In the plan of the original framers of the Bill the principle of Union chargeability had formed an important feature; the system which, three years ago, after a protracted conflict, triumphed in England, was to have been established, in the first instance, in Ireland. But such a scheme in no wise suited the landlords, who, under the lead of the Duke of Wellington, succeeded in "localizing the charge upon the electoral divisions," thus introducing "a quasi-settlement as between the different divisions approximating to settlement as between parishes in England."[1] The clearing of estates thus became a matter of first importance with landlords. Hence the terrible tale of evictions which followed the famine years :—

[1] "History of the Irish Poor-law," p. 288, by Sir George Nicholls.

In 1849 the evicted were 72,065 persons.

1850	„	74,171	„
„ 1851	„	43,449	„
„ 1852	„	32,160	„

When it is borne in mind that relief is left to the discretion of the guardians, and not compulsory, it becomes manifest what a stimulating motive the proprietors had in diminishing the population on their estates to the utmost. Such a regard to its own interest is no disgrace to any class, but it is hardly fair to make out that it springs from a magnanimous unselfishness ; to declare that " it is resistance to an obvious temptation " which discourages leasing and subletting.[1]

---

[1] "What did this law of electoral division rating do ? It gave a premium and an encouragement, even before the famine, for depopulation on every estate. When the famine came, and we had staring us in the face rates from 8s. to 14s. in the pound, landlords and farmers had a fearful dread of labourers coming into or near their farms. If they came into their farms, they were looked upon as if they were wild beasts. . . . The poor were driven into the towns, estates were cleared, and notices to quit were served. If that did not answer, the houses were levelled."—*Quoted by Mr. Butt*, p. 123, from a speech of Serjeant Barry in the House of Commons. I adduce this passage because it alludes to a fact which no doubt is quite true, and often used in argument to combat any change in the actual state of things—the fact, viz. that the labourers are often as harshly treated by the farmers as the latter are by the landlords, and that the labourers are as much entitled to the consideration of Parliament as the tenants. Beyond question they are, and they ought to have it. . But one thing at a time. Because we cannot render complete justice at once, that is no reason why that part of it which it is within our power to afford

It is indeed evident that the proprietors of Ireland dream of a future more fascinating to landlord imagination than anything which exists even in that paradise of landlords, England. They are far from wanting a wretched tenantry, but then the last thing they want is an independent tenantry of rich large farmers, who might easily grow restive.[1] Moderate-sized farms, let without lease, tilled by men who could fairly get along, but who could be squeezed periodically, as circumstances permitted : this is the vision that transports their souls. A pleasant progressive rise in rents, with "hands untied" and full liberty to do as they like with their own, is the fascinating prospect. No doubt Lord Dufferin speaks the truth when he says he does not want the people to emigrate. He says he would like them to turn to other employment, and if capital, and manufactures, and skill would come from heaven, nothing could be more desirable. The great pity is, that capital won't come.

And why will not capital come? The shallow answer is always ready, Because agitation frightens

should be withheld. But this is not the first time that justice to any has been denounced because logically it should lead to justice to all.

[1] "I am by no means disposed to consider the English system of large farms applicable to Ireland. On the contrary, I believe we shall eventually settle down to an average size of farm, as exceptionably suitable as is the gauge of our railways."—*Lord Dufferin*, p. 192.

it away. Supposing it did frighten English and
other capital away, why does not Ireland, like other
countries, develop capital of her own? Besides,
during four-fifths of the last century there was no
more agitation in Ireland than there was in Pom-
peii, but English capital was just as loth to go there
then as it is now. The fact is, there is no more
inducement for capital to go to Ireland than there is
for it to go to Salisbury Plain. English capital has
gone to Ireland for the only two investments which
were open to it, railways and land. Do people
suppose that rich Englishmen will go and start
manufactories in Ireland merely for the novelty of
the thing? Adam Smith's third book of the "Wealth
of Nations" has apparently been written in vain.
The great economist devoted four chapters to this
interesting topic, the growth of capital, or, as he
called, the progress of opulence. He said, to quote
a few sentences from his luminous survey—"As
subsistence is in the nature of things prior to conveniency and luxury, so the industry which procures
the former must be necessarily prior to that which
ministers to the latter. The cultivation and improvement of the country, therefore, which affords
subsistence, must necessarily be prior to the increase
of the town, which furnishes only the means of conveniency and luxury. It is the surplus produce of

the country only, or what is over and above the maintenance of the cultivators, that constitutes the subsistence of the town, which can therefore increase only with the increase of this surplus produce. . . . Neither their employment"—that of the inhabitants of towns—"nor subsistence therefore can augment, but in proportion to the augmentation of the demand from the country for finished work, and this demand can augment only in proportion to the extension of improvement and cultivation."[1] Nothing can be clearer; if the towns have no customers, or only such as are abjectly poor, they cannot thrive. And further : as in the nature of things "subsistence is prior to conveniency and luxury," if wealth does not increase in the country it can, broadly speaking, increase nowhere. Manufactures to be worth anything must be indigenous to the soil, must grow out of the accumulation of small savings, which in time demand on the spot remunerative investment. And this is just what cannot take place in Ireland. Hear what Mr. Marcus Keane says :—"Trade manufactures and industrial occupations require local accumulation of surplus capital in order to the prosperity; and such accumulations are hindered by the general want of security of tenure. Society at large is therefore deeply interested in the protection of the

---

[1] "Wealth of Nations," book iii. cap. 1.

tenant class."[1] I would respectfully invite Lord Dufferin's attention to this passage the next time he feels disposed to lament over the absence of manufactures from Ireland. Mr. Keane says want of security of tenure prevents the accumulation of local capital, and prevents it by making rents rise *pari passu* with improvements, and then confiscating the improvements. In fact the landlords act as a waste pipe, which drains off the surplus capital, which both the great economist and the practical man alike declare to be the indispensable commencement of a manufacturing system. It is well to bear these facts in mind when we are told, as we are constantly, that what Ireland wants is peace, and a "development of her resources."

It thus appears that we may legitimately come to the following conclusions in reference to this question of the present tenure of land in Ireland :—

(1) That insecurity of tenure is a result which the landlords of Ireland advisedly and carefully seek to bring about.

(2) That, whatever other motives may actuate them, a very distinct class interest is preserved and gratified by their present policy.

(3) That that policy, while it places them in a position of extreme ascendency and power, is one

---

[1] "Letter to Colonel Vandeleur," p. 5.

which, at the same time, prevents the accumulation of capital, and keeps the country in that state of chronic poverty which at all times has been the bane of Ireland.

We now come to the paramount right and duty of the State to intervene in such a case as that of Ireland.

We are met at once with outcries at the iniquity of spoliation, confiscation, revolutionary interference with the rights of property. It may be well to cursorily examine how far these alarming exclamations are founded on any principle which gratifies the perpetual *non possumus* of the landlords.

Property is an institution which not only has many defenders, but one which has abundant grounds for defence on its own merits. That the great majority of men will not work unless they are permitted to enjoy the fruits of their work is a proposition which cannot be contested. The question is, how far does this principle go to establish the extreme rights of property in land which are now claimed. It is quite certain no man made the land, although it is equally certain that some man or men made it fertile or fit for production. That man or those men have an indefeasible claim to the fertility and production thence ensuing. I am not at all sure about that, says Lord Dufferin ; in fact I consider Mr. Mill's theory on this point thoroughly unsound. That land is mine, you will observe; and if it suits me to let it to certain persons of the lower classes on terms which we both agree upon, what right has the State to meddle with me, and dictate the conditions of the contract I am willing or able to make? "Hiring land is like hiring a ship. The farmer embarks his capital in another man's field much in the same way as the trader embarks his merchandise in another man's ship. We must not deny the striking analogy between the two cases on the ground that the ship is a manufactured article, but the earth is the gift of God. The land I have bought is probably itself as much a manufactured article as the ship, and the iron or wood of which the ship is built is as much the gift of God as the land. The amount of hire paid for the use of the ship or for the use of the land will be determined by competition. If ships are few and land scarce, freight and rent will rise, and the advantage of the bargain will remain with the owner of the ship and the possessor of the field. An impartial observer may think that the arrangements are unfavourable to the two interests affected by it,—commerce in the one case, farming in the other; but inasmuch as each was a voluntary contract between persons who must be supposed capable of managing their own affairs, any legislative interference to amend the bargain might occasion greater mischief. And here is the conclusion,—if the foregoing illustration be apposite, it follows that the tenant's interest on the farm he hires is quite as limited in its character as the trader's interest in the ship he charters." [1]

Considering the character and position of the writer, it must be admitted that this mode of reasoning is very remarkable. It is difficult to decide whether one shall wonder most at the extraordinary want of precision of thought, or at the absence of all statesmanlike grasp of a complex social problem. "Ships few and land scarce." It is really hard to understand how any cultivated mind could be imposed upon by such a spurious analogy. When land is scarce, can it be increased in quantity? When ships are scarce and are wanted, can they not be increased in any quantity as long as the demand exists? If traders wanted ships as sorely as Irishmen want land, how long does Lord Dufferin suppose they would be without them? And then "the wood and iron the gifts of God." Of course in one sense everything is the gift of God. But human industry causes their appearance in the market, and human industry

---

[1] I give in Appendix C Lord Dufferin's argument *in extenso*.

will supply them, at present at least, and for a good while to come, just in proportion as they are wanted.

Lord Dufferin thinks that the monopolist of a coal mine and the monopolist of a county stand on the same footing. Just let him imagine himself as wanting most urgently both coals and land, and further let him imagine how he would deal with the respective monopolists of the two commodities. He would find the coal merchant perfectly ready to do business with him, and to sell him coals as cheaply as circumstances will admit, as he, the trader, knows quite well the cheaper he sells the more he will sell. Will the monopolist in land receive him in the same manner? Will he not clearly give him to understand that he can and means to do what he likes with his own? Will he not peremptorily show him the conditions on which he intends to transact the matter, and politely tell him if he does not like it he may leave it? In a word, when coal merchants give their customers notice to quit, and tell them they may emigrate for all they care, then, and not till then, will Lord Dufferin's parallel hold good. It is surely passing strange that these elementary considerations in economics should have been overlooked by one of the most respectable and distinguished members of our hereditary senate.

What must be the views and opinions of those members of it who are neither distinguished nor respectable ?

Lord Dufferin distinctly hints at the end of his pamphlet that he has quite demolished Mr. Mill, and this opinion was shared by certain organs of the press. The *Times*, indeed, made a pointed and delicate comparison, and alluded to the waste of time of smashing a butterfly on the wheel, Mr. Mill being the butterfly, and Lord Dufferin the giant who performed the feat. It was an admirable simile, which it is to be hoped the world will not willingly let die. It is quite unnecessary now to interpose in behalf of the smashed butterfly, particularly as the more discerning have quite made up their minds as to who ought in this controversy to be called the butterfly, and who the giant.

As regards Mr. Mill's pamphlet, the essential part of it is simply irrefragable. The State *is* the landlord.

In this dispute between landlord and tenant the State has clearly a right to say, " I acknowledge no rights in either of you but such as are subservient to the general well-being of which I am guardian. I wish the comfort and happiness of both, but neither must make demands and insist upon rights which, however clear and desirable they may appear to you, are distinctly, from the central point of view which I occupy, anti-social. As regards this land, you are and shall be nothing but my tenants, or rather servants. It neither coincides with my interests nor notions of duty that either of you should be wronged or made miserable. Your prosperity and contentment are what I especially seek to secure. Neither shall work the wretchedness of the other. How I shall carry this determination into effect is matter for consideration. Mr. Mill suggests that I should take all the land into my management, and do justice to the husbandmen directly myself. With the profoundest regard for one of the most illustrious of my citizens, I think that great difficulties might be found in working such a scheme. I should have to cover the country with an army of *employés*, and it is not certain that I could, if I would, be always a beneficent landlord under those conditions. But that is no reason why I should not insist that these persons shall be fairly and honestly treated. I also mean to do justice to the landlord. But their class must, as a preliminary, give up all notions that they have a right to say, *l'Etat, c'est moi.*"

It appears to the present writer that the landlord, with an interest in the prosperity of the land, and yet without such paramount powers as to enable

F

him to pay attention to no interests but his own, is
the most convenient person to bridge over the
chasm between the public, personified in the State,
and the actual cultivator of the soil.

This will be done by empowering the solvent
tenant to exact from his landlord the protection
of a lease of say not less than thirty years ; by
making compensation for occupation right a statut-
able right; by making it the landlord's interest to
renew the tenant's lease at some fixed period, say
ten years, before the expiration of such lease ; by
enacting that the landlord who should refuse thus
to renew a lease should pay all rates and taxes for
the last ten years of the unexpired term ; also, that
he shall allow the legal compensation for occupation
right by a *pro rata* deduction from each of the
last ten years' rent. A measure embodying these
or similar provisions would put an end to the
present cruel insecurity, and enable industry and
thrift to reap their just reward.[1]

The practical aim of legislation on this matter
should clearly be to make success or failure in
agricultural pursuits the manifest result of the
agriculturist's own merits or defects. If a farmer is
a fool who cannot learn his business, it is no one's

[1] These suggestions are taken almost literally from the admirable
pamphlet of Mr. Marcus Keane already referred to.

interest to keep him on his farm ; it is the public interest that he should be thrust out of his farm, and that a worthier man should take his place. On the other hand, the good and improving farmer should be protected by walls of adamant from coercion, injustice, or harshness. To say that this is beyond the power of legislation is to say that politics are an impossibility. The good farmer is entitled to every consideration as a faithful soldier in the social army. Not only does he do his duty, but by his example he helps others to do their duty. That such a man should be liable to be robbed of his earnings in the improvements and the capital he has invested in the land, that he should be liable to the odious injustice of being deprived of the post he so worthily fills, is little short of barbarous. The system under which such a thing could occur is nothing less than an organization for disseminating a social blight throughout the country. It stifles industry, energy, and thrift, in their very cradle ; it expunges them from the list of publicly useful virtues.[1]

No class can be a healthy and permanently useful member of the body politic in which energy and intelligence do not meet with their proper reward, and incompetency and sloth their proper chastise-

[1] See Appendix D.

ment. All the community suffers when a grounded discontent pervades any large branch of industry. A "devil's dust" is in such circumstances always mixed with the work they do, and the commodity they produce.

Great calamities and hardships can be borne stoically, if not cheerfully, both by individuals and classes, when it is distinctly seen that no human agency is to blame for them. Earthquakes and tornadoes cause no resentment, frightful as may be their devastations. A cotton famine can reduce four millions of operatives to pauperism and short commons, and the visitation shall be heroically endured when it is clear that no human power could have prevented the catastrophe. But maltreat men by laws and arrangements which only exist because you choose to make them, and then the fiercest passions in the human heart declare war against you. Persist in them after remonstrance and fair warning, then prepare for the day of wrath and vengeance which is surely coming.

III.—THE NATION.

It thus appears that Ireland suffers under two great oppressive grievances : the Established Church and the Tenure of Land. That is to say, that the people of that country are injured both spiritually and materially—in their religious susceptibilities and in their pockets.

But owing to the conditions, especially to the insularity, of the country, these grievances are not merely the grievances of classes, of sections of the community, but of the community itself,—of the Nation, in short.

And these grievances further have been inflicted upon the Irish nation by another nation. The alien Church which casts scorn on the religion of the people was imported into the country, was placed in a position of power and honour with the avowed object of coercing and insulting it. The alien proprietary which holds the land was endowed with that land with the express understanding that the original owners and inhabitants should be carefully expelled from it.[1] And both these things were done, not by a powerful unscrupulous class in the country itself, but by a foreign power which, by reason of

---

[1] The attempt of the English Government to exterminate the native Irish in the reign of Elizabeth has lately had justice done to it by Mr. Froude, in his 10th vol. chap. 24. " The English nation," he says, " was shuddering over the atrocities of the Duke of Alva. The children in the nurseries were being inflamed to patriotic rage and madness by the tales of Spanish tyranny. Yet Alva's bloody sword never touched the young, the defenceless, or those whose sex even dogs can recognise and respect. Sir Peter Carew had been seen murdering women and children, and babies that had scarcely left the breast. But Sir Peter Carew was not called to answer for his conduct, and remained in favour with the deputy. Gilbert, who was left in command at Kilmalock, was illustrating yet more signally the same tendency. . . . . He regarded himself as dealing rather with savage beasts than with human beings, and when he tracked them to their dens he strangled the cubs, and rooted out the entire broods." Mr. Froude adds that this method of treatment had the disadvantage that it must be carried out to the last extremity, or it ought not to be tried at all, and there were obvious difficulties in the way of doing it thoroughly.

Therefore the next effort on the part of the English to rid themselves of the Irish took the form of transplanting. James I. did this for Ulster, and was very successful. Cromwell tried to continue his work in Leinster and Munster, and failed in comparison. Those who wish to obtain a clear notion of what literally without any exaggeration is one of the most awful chapters in human annals, should read the " Cromwellian Settlement of Ireland," by Mr. John Prendergast. " Connaught was selected for the habitation of all the Irish nation by reason of its being surrounded by the sea and the Shannon all but ten miles, and the whole easily made into one by a line of forts. To further secure the imprisonment of the nation, and to cut them off from relief by sea, a belt of four miles wide, commencing one mile west of Sligo, and so winding along the sea-coast and the Shannon, was reserved by the Act (27th September, 1653) from being let out to the Irish, and was to be given to the soldiery to plant. . . . . There they were to dwell without entering a walled town, or coming within five miles of some on pain of death. All were to remove thither by the 1st of May, 1654, at latest, under pain of being put to death by sentence of a court

differences of race, language, and religion, was animated towards it with the intensest forms of hatred and cruelty.

of military officers if found after that date on the English side of the Shannon."—*Cromwellian Settlement of Ireland*, pp. 29, 30. This transplanting work, as it was called, gave a good deal of trouble to Cromwell's officers, who declared : "It is the nature of this people to be rebellious, and they have been so-much the more disposed to it, having been highly exasperated by the transplanting work."—*Ibid.* p. 50. They fliuched not, however.

"I have only to acquaint you that the time prescribed for the transplanting of the Irish proprietors, and those that have been in arms and abettors of the rebellion, being near at hand, the officers are resolved to fill the gaols and seize them, by which this bloody people will know that they (the officers) are not degenerated from English principles. Though I presume we shall be very tender of hanging, except leading men, yet we shall make no scruple of sending them to the West Indies, where they will serve for planters."—*Ibid.* p. 52. Still hanging had to be resorted to, and more than one was hanged with placards back and front, "For not transplanting."

But the adventurers themselves soon found it to their interest not to push the transplanting too far ; and "as the impossibility of getting English tenants grew more evident, and the urgent want of tillage increased, the officers in Limerick, Cork, Kerry, and other counties gave general orders, giving dispensation from the necessity of planting with English tenants, and liberty to take Irish, provided they were not proprietors or swordsmen. . . . . On the 1st of June, 1655, the Commissioners for the Affairs of Ireland, Fleetwood Lord Deputy, one of them, being then at Limerick, discovered this fraud, and issued a peremptory order, revoking all former dispensations for English proprietors to plant with Irish tenants, and then enjoined upon the Governor of Limerick and all other officers the removing of the proprietors thus sheltered and their families into Connaught, on or before that day three weeks." Still many of the English officers connived at the breaking of this order, and drew down upon themselves this severe rebuke from Fleetwood : "I do hereby order and declare that if any officer or soldier under my command shall offend by neglect of his duty in searching for and apprehending all such persons as, by the declaration of 30th November, are to transplant themselves into Connaught, or by enter-

Hence Ireland complains, not only of this or that grievance or injustice, but of a grand synthesis of grievances which sums them all up, which gives an additional weight to each by throwing it into the grand total which figures under the head of national wrongs.

I well know the impatience which even an allusion to this subject excites in England. The notion of Irish nationality is regarded as partly wicked, and partly insane. " What do the Irish want ?" it is asked ; "why cannot they let by-gones be by-gones ? We all know they were badly treated once ; but that is all over now, and occurred long ago. Why cannot they accept thankfully and proudly the magnificent privileges of British citizenship now offered them ? The whole agitation is dishonest and unreal."

It would be hardly worth while to remind the Englishmen who hold this view, with what scorn they treat similar language in the mouth of a Bourbon or a Hapsburg, or even of a North Ame-

---

taining them as tenants on his land, as servants under him, he shall be punished by the articles of war as negligent of his duty, according to the merit of such his neglect."—*Cromwellian Settlement of Ireland*, pp. 131-33. Again the territory commonly called " the five counties " was ordered to be *wholly* cleared of Irish Papists by the 1st of May, 1655, on pain of being taken as spies, and proceeded with before a court martial. But difficulties supervened in carrying out this scheme.

rican Republican, or how effusely their sympathy is given to the all and sundry of rebels, provided they are not their subjects. The important thing is to convince them of the very substantial reasons which lead the Irish to take so very different a view of their connexion with England from that which they do themselves.

Two preliminary remarks are here to be made. (1) That conquest, so far from being an exception in the history of States, is, on the contrary, the rule. As Guizot has said, " L'origine de tous les gouvernements, c'est la force." The fact that Ireland was conquered by England is no peculiarity. England, France, Spain, Italy were all conquered, and have all got over their conquest.

(2) Nations have long memories, and their memories are long in proportion to their endowments and cultivation. The English people live in their past as much as any people. Happily for them it is a past in which they can, for the most part, feel a just pride. Crecy, Poitiers, and Agincourt are names which still occasionally send a thrill through most men whose limbs were made in England. The triumph over the Spanish Armada has not lost a particle of lustre after nearly three centuries in English eyes. The heroes who have spread the fame of England, whether on sea or

land, or in arts or in science, are "familiar in our mouths as household words." There is a certain class of by-gones which we should be the last to let fade away.

And now let us see how these two remarks apply to the special case of Ireland.

Why should Ireland be for ever lamenting her conquest, when we see it is the common fate of nations sooner or later? The answer is, that the conquest of Ireland was a vulgar event enough; it is the state of things that has supervened on that conquest which is grave and almost without parallel. France took Alsace and Strasbourg with every circumstance of treachery and cruelty only a few years before William and his generals completed the final subduing of Ireland. Yet Alsace is a contented French province, and Ireland is in chronic insurrection. Strasbourg is as loyal to France as any town in the Empire; Cork, and even Dublin, are filled with men whose one idea is how to break loose from and injure England. The explanation of the difference is, that in the one case the wounds of conquest have been allowed to heal, while in the other they have been kept open and bleeding.

It is not because Ireland was conquered two centuries ago that she is bitter, moody, and wretched now; but because the sharp and cruel effects of that conquest are cutting and maiming her still,—because her daily experience rehearses for her not the act of conquest, but the division of the spoil which followed it. It would, no doubt, require a very rose-coloured present to obliterate from her memory her terrible past. But her present, instead of being rose-coloured, is as gloomy as in these modern humane days it well can be. She certainly is not scourged, and shot, and hanged as formerly; but, *mutatis mutandis*, things are not so very different with her from what they were in the last or in the seventeenth century. Her people were then told they might go to "hell or Connaught;" they are now told they may go, if they will be so good, to America. Fire and sword were the weapons of those days; evictions and doctrines about the sacred rights of property are the weapons of ours. The means, no doubt, are very different, but the object is precisely the same.

What did the conquest do to Ireland? It gave her churches and their endowments to an alien clergy; it gave her land to an alien proprietary. And what does the actual policy do but jealously continue and confirm the state of matters established by the conquest? The battle of the Boyne seems an historical event, antiquated enough to Englishmen. But events still occur in Ireland which bring back in all their vividness the results it produced. There is a well-known case in the north of Ireland at this moment, in which the proprietor has deliberately turned a large tract of country to waste sooner than come to terms with his tenants. Thus the present forms one web with the past. And who always appears to the Irish mind in the character of a fell sister, spinning this abhorred thread of wretchedness? Who supports the landlords? Who supports, or at least it happily may soon be asked, Who has hitherto supported the Church? Who covers the country with a powerful army? Who crowds the prisons with political prisoners?[1] The humiliating answer is

---

[1] Few persons in England realize the perfectly frightful insecurity of personal liberty in Ireland at the present moment. In spite of all the honeyed talk as to the moderation with which the exceptional powers given to the Irish Executive are used, it remains a fact that people are almost daily and nightly quietly kidnapped and carried off to prison on mere suspicion, and are kept there without trial or even accusation for periods sometimes amounting to two years, and then discharged without even the pretence of a crime being alleged against them. Lately the *lettre de cachet* system, as it is justly called in Ireland, has been developed into almost a complete likeness to its great original under Louis XV. The plan is now adopted of concealing the names of the captives.

"During the past few days a large number of arrests on charges of complicity in the Fenian conspiracy, and under the suspension of the Habeas Corpus Act, have been made in Dublin by the detective police. *In every instance the utmost secrecy was observed by the authorities,* and

that England does; and that — saving a little harshness the less in details—the policy is identical with that which has obtained for centuries.

it was only by the complaints of the relatives and friends of the prisoners that the facts became known. Amongst those arrested was the brother of one of the Fenian prisoners, who died in prison whilst undergoing a term of imprisonment inflicted on him at one of the recent commissions for an alleged connexion with Fenianism. We doubt the wisdom of the course observed by the authorities in preserving such mystery as to the facts of these arrests."—*Freeman.*

"We understand that the detective officers have recently arrested a number of persons on warrants signed by the Lord Lieutenant, under the Habeas Corpus Suspension Act. The authorities are extremely reticent *with reference to these arrests, and we have not been able to learn the names of any of the persons taken into custody.* It is said, however, that one is the brother of a Fenian prisoner who died in prison a short time ago."—*Express.*

"Merely by indirect means have we been made aware of the arrests that have taken place in the city of the past fortnight. Though in some cases the evidence was strong against the parties, in others that suspicion only justified the arrests, the detectives were particularly reticent as to the exact details, *and it could be found out only with difficulty that captures had been effected.* In one case it has been ascertained that the brother of one already undergoing imprisonment has been sent to jail."—*Irish Times.*

"It is stated that several persons have been arrested within the last month in this city, under the Habeas Corpus Suspension Act, for complicity in the Fenian conspiracy, by the detective police. Unusual official reticence has been of late observed by the authorities, and we have been unable to obtain the names of those arrested through the usual channel of information. Doubtless the authorities have good reason for their unusual secrecy in reference to their prisoners. The brother of a man who lately died while in custody on a charge of Fenianism is said to be amongst those arrested."—*Saunders News Letter.*

It should also be remembered that the nominal imprisonment which Messrs. Sullivan and Pigott are undergoing is really penal servitude. Their confinement is solitary for twenty-two hours out of the twenty-four. They have not the use of either pen, ink, and paper, nor of books. They may not receive, not answer letters. The most trifling

That policy is the coercion of Ireland at the pleasure, and for the supposed benefit, of England. People must have a strange conception of human nature in general, and of Irish nature in particular, if they wonder that bitter national antipathy is the result of such a policy. It argues a singular dulness of imagination not to be able to realize the intense national spirit of antagonism and hatred which must be evoked by perpetual thwarting, compression and oppression. An Irishman, looking up the vista of his country's history, sees one recurring fact always prominent, always crushing him and his country as with the weight of mountains. From the all but mythic twilight of the Middle Ages down to the year of grace 1868, the same great shadow is thrown across his land from the same great object. Under this shadow he has cowered and shuddered for ages, it has ever filled his horizon, and been

"A looming bastion fringed with fire,"

with fire which could descend and burn him and his like flax.[1] And because he dreads the fire, because

---

infringement of prison rules (such as the most trivial remark to another prisoner) is punished by a bread and water diet, and the black hole.

[1] The bland way in which Englishmen agree to think no more about the atrocities they have committed in Ireland would be quite amusing

his mind is still full of horror and agony at the terrible heat of it, he is disaffected—he has not that proper spirit of loyalty which Englishmen admire.

The misfortune is that this condition of Irish feeling is most imperfectly realized and appreciated in this country. It is still the real or supposed interest, or at least the object, of many in this country, to represent the prevalent sentiments of Irishmen as something very different from this; to assert that all this emigration and noisy disaffection means nothing after all, that the people are sound and loyal at heart; and the desired moral follows of course: "Don't meddle, don't interfere, let well alone; for your life don't listen to any 'tampering' with the rights of property; and as for a national spirit, treat it with the contempt such an absurd figment deserves." This advice has been followed too long, and has already cost far too dear. To those who know Ireland and her history its in-

---

were it in connexion with any less terrible subject. Every school-girl taught to shudder at the wickedness of the French Revolutionists, and the crimes of the Reign of Terror are carefully instilled into the youthful mind to impress it with a due abhorrence of republicans, and the excesses they by nature are sure to be guilty of. The Reign of Terror which a chaste and pious George III. and a heaven-born minister suffered to exist in Ireland, is conveniently forgotten. Robespierre and St. Just are held up as monsters; but Lieutenant Helpenstall and Judkin Fitzgerald, wretches compared with whom the French Conventionists were almost humanitarians, are not even mentioned.

sidious malice is plain enough; but it can hardly be expected that the busy and not over-studious British people will so readily detect the fallacy of the specious counsel. The counsel, being interpreted, means shortly this: " Take no notice of the real Ireland, Catholic, Celtic Ireland; think only of the sham Ireland, the exotic Ireland we have planted there, the Ireland of Protestantism and landlords." The result is that the mind of the English nation is never brought into contact with the facts of the political problem which it vitally concerns the English nation to solve. Hence flow the most lamentable delusions, the most ill-founded hopes, followed by fierce gusts of disappointment. While the hallucination lasts that Irish disaffection arises from a foreign element let loose upon us by the disbanding of the American armies, that artful agitators who play upon the passions of an excitable people are the source of our trouble, truly remedial measures for Ireland are impossible, simply because the gigantic proportions of the task before us are not even suspected. The first necessity for Englishmen is to get thoroughly and solemnly convinced that large numbers of Irishmen hate them and their country with the bitterest hatred that it is possible to conceive; and the next is to admit that Englishmen have done very much to deserve that hatred.[1] It will not do, in the old silly ostrich fashion, to ignore or despise this hatred ; a fact, indeed, of daily increasing difficulty. The hatred is one of the conditions of the problem with which we have to deal. As we cannot sink Ireland in the sea, and are determined to keep her to ourselves, it is clear that remedial measures, very different from any yet propounded, are required to make a United Kingdom a reality instead of a constitutional fiction. As Mr. Mill says, our difficulty is a difficulty of understanding, of seeing the facts as they are. And yet our recent experience encourages us to make any effort to overcome this difficulty. After three centuries of blindness our eyes have been opened to the iniquity of the Established Church. And already the good fruit is beginning to grow in Ireland. In time we may

---

[1] Within the last few weeks all this is at an end. Not only Irish disaffection but Irish grievances have been suddenly, and as if by magic, removed by the simple method of driving the Prince and Princess of Wales round and about Dublin, and by their appearance at the Punchestown races. If this is really the fact, what are we to think of a Government which did not avail itself of so easy a remedy for rebellion and disaffection before? It was not Lord Strathnairn and an army, but the Heir Apparent and a carriage and four, that ought to have been sent to Ireland. It is difficult to maintain one's gravity over such a delusion— if, indeed, it is a delusion which deludes anybody. Why did not the special correspondent of the *Times* at once restore to the Royal Family their anciently supposed power of cure by touching for the evil? or why not make the Prince heal all the halt and the blind in the Dublin hospitals with a wave of his finger? Moral miracles quite as great are ascribed to him.

see the other iniquities. We have seen the wrong of ecclesiastical ascendency; let it be hoped we shall soon see the wrong of lay—that is, of landlord ascendency, and generally of English and British Parliament ascendency.

As regards the native schemes of separate legislatures, Irish Republic, and what not, I confess that to me, they appear truly to bear the character of *ægri somnia*, the sick dreams of poor Ireland half delirious through English coldness and oppression. I do not recommend that the dreams of delirium should be gratified, but that its cause should be removed. Whatever may prove the ultimately wise method to do this, I am sure the obsolete cruelties once practised on the insane will effect no good. Strait waistcoat, scourging, and starving, as curative means are long out of date. We had better have a care, or we may drive the semi-delirium into settled madness. As we see, symptoms of homicidal mania are already not wanting.

The first requisite, then, for the real pacification of Ireland, with all deference I would say, is a new heart and a new mind on the part of England towards her, a new conviction of her sad case, and of our still sadder responsibility for it. A first-rate remedial measure would be a compulsory study of Irish history by every Englishman who could read.

Englishmen would then see what they have done, or rather suffered to be done, in their name, and more adequately realize how much they have now to undo.

When the national conscience is once fairly aroused on this subject, the English public will find itself in a new world. The patronising way in which England, the wrong-doer, now so frequently and magnanimously offers to condone and forget the past, will, it may be hoped, be laid aside. Especially may a change be expected in the tone of allusions to, and estimates of, the Union. One of the most nefarious transactions in human history, and now proved calamitous in its effects, will probably cease to be regarded as a venerable covenant with which it is impious to meddle. What changes or additions will be made to the terms of union, it is the business of practical statesmen to consider. An autumn session of the Irish representatives in Dublin, invested with considerable powers of local government, is one scheme, and well worth considering. An occasional session of the Imperial Parliament in Ireland —say once in three years—is another, and the suggestion of a thinker who knows Ireland as few do, Mr. Goldwin Smith ; who would also substitute for a single central assembly in Dublin for the whole of Ireland four provincial councils in the

four provinces. The time for discussing these pro-
posals has unhappily not yet arrived ; but the first
stirrings of statesmanship among us will inevitably
bring them rapidly to the front. We cannot continue in the present unendurable rule of imbecile
routine ; a ceaseless proclamation of our own political incompetence has ceased to impose on Ireland,
and cannot much longer impose on ourselves. It
rests with the energetic, intelligent, and unselfish
portion of the English nation very earnestly to see
to it that the republic receive no further detriment.

Whether a great and crushing Nemesis is destined
to overtake this nation in consequence of her treatment of Ireland is what the future only can dis-
close. Nothing but the blindness of stupidity can
refuse to see that perils of an unprecedented order
are threatening us. They may burst upon our
heads amid the not over-sorrowful spectators of
the civilized world. They may pass over and leave
us to our old ways. We are strong, tenacious, and
rich. We can still do much evil. Other countries
are slow even to attempt the punishment of such
imperial wrong-doers. The poor Irish must and
do see that they are weak as rushes before us.
Frenchmen, Americans, Russians have all got their
hands full enough of troubles to leave us alone
without pressing necessity of interference. That

necessity may never arrive. We are in a position neither to fear God nor to regard man, if we choose to avail ourselves of it. But no! not yet will a patriotic Englishman think such an awful future destined for his country. Righteous men there still are among us, great and numerous as are our sins. Not yet can we believe that the countrymen of Hampden, of Milton, and Sydney are all unworthy of their sires. Even yet may this nation be touched by the Ithuriel spear of conscience, and burn with a holy ardour to do what is lawful and right. We will hope in the virtue and valour of the coming time, of a new era, of that future which shall be all the brighter that the past was base.

APPENDIX.

Appendix A, referred to at P. 34.

On the estate of the Marquis of Lansdowne, in Kerry, an order of this nature had been issued. I will not attempt to weaken the effect of the narrative of "S. G. O." by any paraphrase :—

"On the estate of the Marquis of Lansdowne there lived, a few months ago, a man and his wife, Michael and Judith Donoghue ; they lived in the house of one Casey. An order had gone forth on the estate (a common order in Ireland) that no tenant is to admit any lodger into his house. This was a general order. It appears, however, that sometimes special orders are given, having regard to particular individuals. The Donoghues had a nephew, one Denis Shea. This boy had no father living. He had lived with a grandmother who had been turned out of her holding for harbouring him. Denis Shea was twelve years old—a child of decidedly dishonest habits. Orders were given by the driver of this estate that this child should not be harboured upon it. This young Cain, thus branded and prosecuted, being a thief—he had stolen a shilling, a hen, and done many other such crimes as a neglected twelve-year-old famishing child will do—wandered about. One night he came to his aunt Donoghue, who lodged with Casey. He had the hen with him.

"Casey told his lodgers not to 'allow him in the house,' as the agent's drivers had given orders about it. The woman, the child's aunt, took up a pike or pitchfork and struck him down with it; the child was crying at the time. The man Donoghue, his uncle, with a cord tied the child's hands behind his back. The poor child after a while crawls or staggers to the door of one Sullivan, and tried to get in there. The maid of Sullivan called to Donoghue to take him away. This he did; but he afterwards returned, with his hands still tied behind his back. Donoghue had already beaten him severely. The child seeks refuge in other cabins, but is pursued by his character—he was so bad a boy, the fear of the agent and the driver—all were forbidden to shelter him. He is brought back by some neighbours, in the night, to Casey's, where his uncle and aunt lived. The said neighbours tried to force the sinking child in upon his relations. There is a struggle at the door. The child was heard asking some one to put him upright. In the morning there is blood upon the threshold. The child is stiff dead—a corpse with its arms tied; around it every mark of a last fearful struggle for shelter—food—the common rights of humanity.

"The Donoghues were tried at the late Kerry Assizes. It was, morally, a clear case of murder; but it was said, or believed, that these Donoghues acted not in malice to the child, but under a sort of sense of self-preservation; that they felt to admit him was to become wanderers themselves. They were indicted for manslaughter, and found guilty."

APPENDIX B, REFERRED TO AT P. 46.

The actual position of the tenant in Ireland with regard to compensation for improvements:—

"In Ireland, when a lease is likely to fall in and a new one is not agreed upon, or when a tenant is improvident, the land is run out—that is, the pasture land is mown and the arable land is cropped till nothing more can be got out of it. Supposing you were entering on a farm of this description, as I did on one I purchased twelve years ago, you must either buy manure, or hay, corn, linseed-cake, &c., to feed cattle and sheep, in order to make it : for two or three years, according to the nature of the land and your own knowledge of farming, you would actually sustain a loss; as your land came round you would have to consider whether it would pay you better to be a grazier, laying all your farm gradually down in grass, or whether you would farm on the four-course system, growing cereals, green crops, clover, &c. If you did the latter, there would always be a considerable portion of your land which had been manured the previous year, or the year before that; and if you were a judicious manager, and cultivated your land as you ought, your farm would be worth from ten shillings to a pound an acre more than when you got it ; and without reckoning good-will at all, the unexhausted manure in the land should be worth several pounds an acre. Now, under the head of permanent improvements, you would not be entitled to sixpence if you were ejected. In some counties in England you would be liberally paid, but at present in Ireland nothing is allowed, which I think accounts for a great deal of bad husbandry. But supposing you turned the greater portion of your farm into grass, and after feeding sheep and young cattle found your land so improved that it would fatten good-sized beasts, you would have spent many years in arriving at such a pitch of perfection, and expended a great deal of money in top-dressing, &c. : you would at least have doubled the value of your farm, as I have in several instances doubled the value of land I have purchased. Well, when you had done this, if you were ejected, you would not be entitled to anything, under any law past or projected ; your landlord would take the farm, which you had received in an exhausted state, and which you had rendered fertile and profitable, and would either keep it in his own hands, or let it for perhaps two pounds an acre more than you paid or than any one would give when you took it, and you would have to go elsewhere. Can any one wonder that Irish tenants will not be satisfied with an Act which would allow injustice of this kind to be perpetrated !"—*A Saxon's Remedy for Irish Discontent*, p. 357, one of the very best books yet written on the subject, by a practical and candid thinker who is evidently master of it.

"A tenant, on the other hand, is a person who does not possess land, but who hires the use of it. He embarks his capital in another man's field, much in the same way as a trader embarks his merchandise in another man's ship. Experience teaches him that by expending a certain amount of labour and capital in the cultivation of the soil he is able, within a limited period, to get back from it, not only the original capital he had expended, but also a profitable rate of interest upon that capital. What rate that interest may reach will depend on his own skill and discretion, just as the trader's profits will depend on the judgment with which he sorts his cargo or selects his port. In either case, the amount of hire paid for the use of the ship or for the use of the land will be determined by competition, and will affect the balance of gain or loss on both transactions. If ships are few and land is scarce, freight and rent will rise, and the rise of each will in a great measure be regulated by the disproportion of ships to goods and of farmers to farms. But the rate of freight or the amount of rent are not the only circumstances which will affect the profits of either speculator. In the case of the trader, all will depend on his goods being landed at the port he intended, whilst the most promising expectations of the agriculturist may be ruined unless he retain possession of the land he occupies for a definite period. A clear understanding, therefore, ought to exist in both cases between the parties interested, as to the course of the ship and the duration of the tenancy. The shipowner may want to send his vessel to one port and the trader his goods to another, just as the proprietor of an estate may wish to let his land for one term and the tenant to hire it for another. The definitive arrangement will depend upon the respective necessities of the contracting parties and the balance of competition. On the previous supposition that ships are few and land scarce, the advantage of the bargain will remain with the owner of the ship and the possessor of the field ; the one consenting to call at the desired port, unforeseen contingencies permitting—the other agreeing to let his land on such conditions as may be most suitable to his ulterior views. Both arrangements may be thought by the impartial observer unfavourable to the two interests affected by it—the one to commerce, the other to agriculture; but, inasmuch as each was a voluntary contract between persons who must be supposed capable of managing their own affairs, any legislative interference to amend the bargain might occasion greater mischief. For instance, a law requiring the ship to call at certain ports, or the landlord to let his land for what he might consider a longer term than was desirable, would be a grievance to both shipowner and landowner; they would probably protect themselves either by refusing to carry the goods and to let the field, or by raising the rate of their freight and rent. This result would suit neither merchant nor farmer. Parliament might again intervene, and not only lay down the plan of the voyage and the duration of the tenure, but might impose a specified scale of freights and rents, and declare the shipowner incapable of freighting his own ship and the landlord of tilling his own land. But so violent an interference with the rights of property would be unjust, impracticable, and obviously productive of greater evils than those it was intended to remedy.

" If the foregoing illustration be apposite, it follows that the tenant's interest in the farm he hires is quite as limited in its character as the trader's interest in the ship he charters. The voyage concluded, the lease expired, both ship and field revert to their respective owners.

" It is hardly reasonable to deny the analogy on the ground that the ship is a manufactured article, but the earth is the gift of God. The land I have bought is probably itself as much a manufactured article as the ship, and the iron or wood of which the ship is built is as much the gift of God as the land: the labour or enterprise by which the land has been rendered valuable is as clearly represented by the money I gave for it as the industry and ingenuity exercised on its construction is represented by the price the owner has paid for the ship. It is true, the country of which my estate is part belongs to the nation, and consequently my property in that estate is overridden by the imperial rights of the commonwealth. But this fact cannot invest the individual who may happen to hire my land, *when once his tenancy is terminated, either by lapse of time or by the violation of his contract,* with any peculiar rights in excess of those which may be inherent to the community at large."—*Irish Emigration and the Tenure of Land in Ireland,* by Lord Dufferin, pp. 184—187.

Appendix D, referred to at P. 67.

" Perhaps the landlord party will try to get rid of my proposition, or any similar one, by saying they will consent to an Act that shall give the tenant compensation for permanent improvements, by which, of course, they mean drainage, farm-buildings, &c. Now a measure of this kind would only be a palliative. Of course it would be accepted ; but agitation would recommence, for Irish tenants would not be satisfied. Allowances for improvements mean allowances when the tenant is ejected ; and every Englishman who reads this may rest assured that the great body of the Irish tenantry, Protestant and Catholic, will not rest contented as long as they are liable to be put out of their holdings for any cause except the non-payment of rent and neglect of the usual covenants necessary for the maintenance of the property in good condition."—*A Saxon's Remedy for Irish Discontent.*

LONDON : R. CLAY, SON, AND TAYLOR, PRINTERS.

www.ingramcontent.com/pod-product-compliance
Lightning Source LLC
Chambersburg PA
CBHW021411090426
42742CB00009B/1100